Renovating the Victorian House

To the Cathcarts –
thanks again for welcoming
me into your lovely home. The
photographs, as you will see,
are lovely additions to this book
– Kathy Knight

Renovating the Victorian House

Katherine Knight Rusk

101 Productions
San Francisco

TECHNICAL DRAWINGS Nancie West Swanberg
COVER AND TEXT DESIGN Patricia Glover

Printed and bound in the United States of America.

Distributed to the book trade in the United States by Charles Scribner's Sons, New York.

Published by 101 Productions
834 Mission Street
San Francisco, California 94103

1 3 5 7 9 11 13 15 17 19 20 18 16 14 12 10 8 6 4 2
Library of Congress Cataloging in Publication Data

Rusk, Katherine Wright
Renovating the Victorian house

Bibliography: p.
Includes index.
I. Dwellings--Remodeling. 2. Architecture, Victorian--Conservation and restoration. I. Title.
TH4816.R86 1982 643'.7 82-12397
ISBN 0-89286-187-8 pbk
ISBN 0-89286-217-3

COVER NOTES

FRONT COVER A bay-windowed Italianate in San Francisco, designed in the late 19th century by architect Henry Geilfuss and later converted into apartments. Renovated in 1980 by architect Roy Killeen. The free-standing colonnettes around the window are a rare detail. Photograph: Rik Olson.

BACK COVER Another San Francisco Italianate sorely in need of repair. Photograph: Patricia Glover.

Contents

Introduction

The historic preservation movement is growing, and house renovation has become a nationwide fad. People are moving back into the core cities where Victorian houses are plentiful, drawn by an appreciation for America's heritage and spurred by exorbitant commuting costs.

A well-made house of natural materials is a welcome departure from the shoddy, synthetic techniques that characterize much modern construction. Even the two-by-fours in a Victorian house are 2 inches by 4 inches! Economically, also, older homes are a good bet. Victorian houses can still be purchased for a fraction of their renovated value. Federal and state governments offer tax benefits and subsidies in certain cases. And, in this era of volatile economics, financing an old home has become easier than obtaining a mortgage on a new dwelling.

Emotional attachments to Victorian homes can be strong as well. Some people have a nostalgia for the house where grandma lived. Others love the lofty ceilings, spacious rooms, and majestic fireplaces of those grand madams.

House renovation isn't for everyone, however, and there are compelling reasons to avoid it. Weigh them carefully. Rehabilitating a Victorian home takes a lot of time, work, and (no matter how much labor you do yourself) a certain amount of money. Renovation never proceeds as quickly as you planned, and, during the process, you will find yourself wistfully coveting your friends' new (and completed) homes.

What you have envisioned as a project soon becomes a way of life. Renovating an old home means dirt under your fingernails (what's left of them); tools, nails, and electrical paraphernalia bulging from your purse or pockets; sawdust in your hair; paint specks on your glasses; and plaster dust everywhere. It means returning home to such unpleasant surprises as several inches of water on the kitchen floor. It often means poor plumbing, inadequate wiring, and nonexistent heating. Treasure hunts for rare fixtures and hardware can be fun, but if you have to scour a dozen plumbing stores before you find that essential, obsolete washer, the treasure hunt disintegrates into a frustrating search for the holy grail.

Consider the challenge one Maryland couple faced:

> Soon after we were married, Nancy and I had the opportunity to purchase an old house and a few acres. The house had not been cared for properly for about 15 years, and needless to say, was in rather poor condition. There was no heating or septic system, the water pipes had all burst during previous winters, only three electrical outlets worked, windows had been broken, and the front porch floor had rotted into oblivion. The lawn had become a tall pasture and the shrub border consisted of lilacs supported primarily by honeysuckle, brambles, and poison ivy.
>
> In thinking back, I believe the main reason we fell in love with this place was because it had been neglected so long.[1]

Definitely crazy. But, then, when you're hooked, you're hooked.

A single volume cannot begin to relate everything there is to know about Victorian houses and house renovation. I hope you will use this book as a springboard and consult the resources mentioned throughout for in-depth study in areas of interest to you.

ACKNOWLEDGMENTS

This book is the outgrowth of the many hours I have spent digging for answers to the problems and tasks I faced renovating my own Victorian-era houses. During this quest, I not only gathered a wealth of knowledge, but also came to know an even greater wealth of people who love and have owned or worked on Victorian-era houses. These people—grandfathers of friends, acquaintances of acquaintances, retired craftspersons—have imparted to me tidbits of knowledge and nearly lost skills. They have made this book possible and unique.

The book wouldn't be complete without the input of Sean Fitzpatrick, a contractor who has worked on scores of old-house renovations in central and northern California. Sean's comments and philosophy run throughout this book, from the analyses of Victorian social customs to demolition techniques to wallpapering. Specifically, his expertise is the foundation for the chapters on tools; siding; working with a contractor; appeasing the building inspector; and roofs, gutters, and eaves. He also made significant contributions to the chapters on plumbing, electricity, heating, painting, structural integrity, and moving houses.

Despite my six years of renovation experience, I learned a lot working with Sean on this book. He has gently mocked me at times for not knowing about a particular material or technique—or for spending hours on a task that would have taken him only a few minutes. More than once I learned from him—after the fact—how I should have done a particular job. Behind the respect I have developed for Sean is my conviction that, even though he earns his living renovating old houses, his motivation emanates from a commitment to doing a job the right way—a commitment tempered with a genuine appreciation of old materials and craftsmanship and a sensitivity to preserving each house's individual character and heritage. If you work with a pro, don't settle for less.

Many of the photographs in this book were taken by John Burrows of Bradbury and Bradbury Wallpapers. I feel a deep gratitude towards John and towards Bruce Bradbury (mentor of Bradbury and Bradbury and self-proclaimed Victorian wallpaper fanatic) for their information and assistance.

I would also like to thank Mac the Antique Plumber (who could always manage to find that obsolete washer); Ken Marr of Marr-Schaefer Associates; Michael Mattis, editor of the "California Life" section of the *Sacramento Bee*; Dave Whitlock, proprietor of the Moulding Mart; Marion Mitchell-Wilson of the California State Office of Historic Preservation; David R. Simmons of the Insurance Information Institute; Nancie West Swanberg, the book's illustrator; Frederick W. Stephenson; and Brian Reardon, alias Jack the Stripper.

Thanks also to Kathryn Lehman, my typist and also my oldest friend, and to John A. Tosney, my husband, for their support and infinite patience; and to Ted Knight, my father, who printed the photographs for the book.

And finally, I wish to dedicate this book to my dear friend, Lori McMahan, who has given me motivation and glasses of wine—and whose beautifully renovated 1889 Queen Anne home has been a constant inspiration to me.